NURSE COLORING BOOK FOR KIDS

Ages 4-10

52 CUTE COLORING PAGES

This Books Belongs To

Color Test Page

THANK YOU!

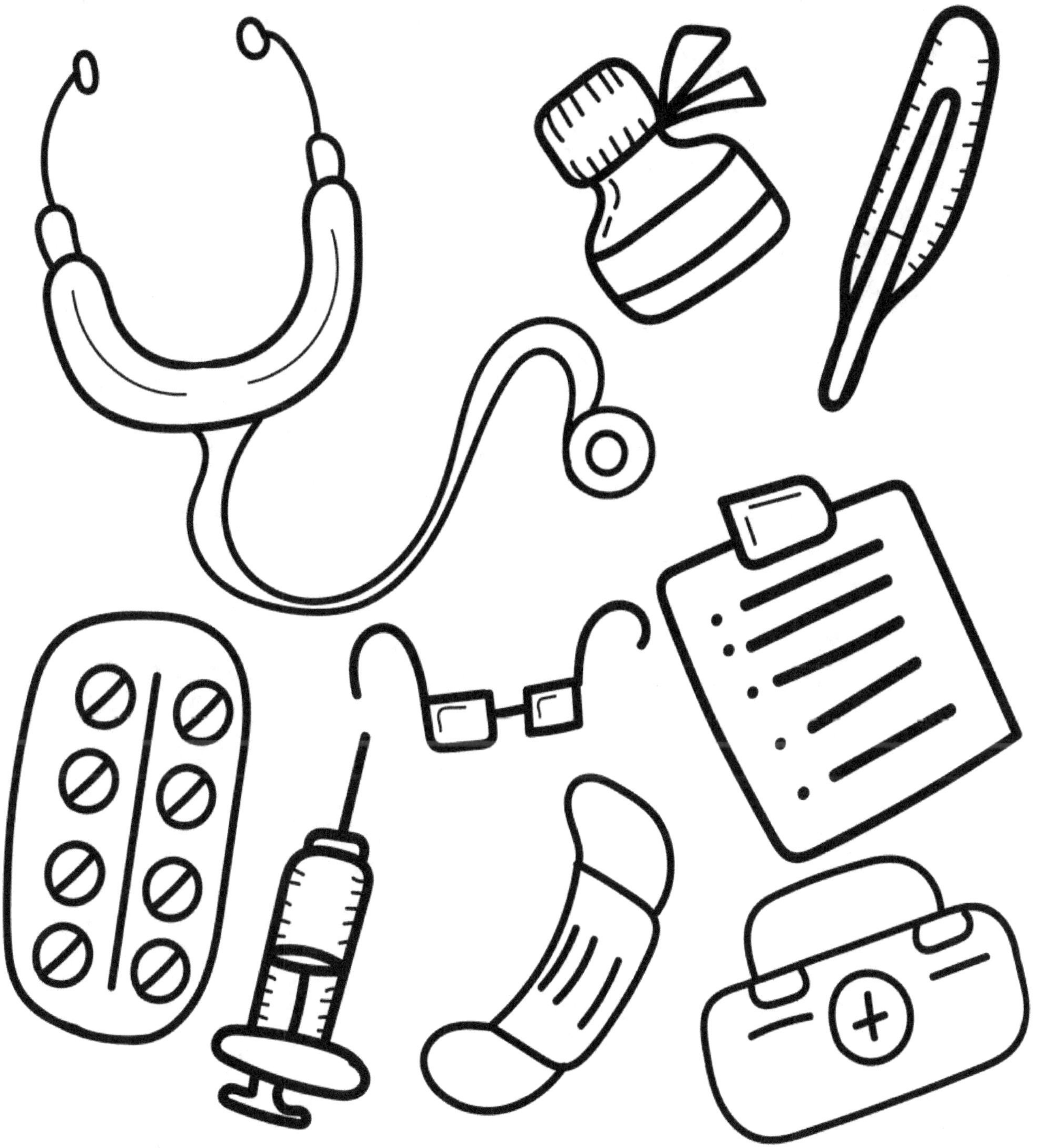

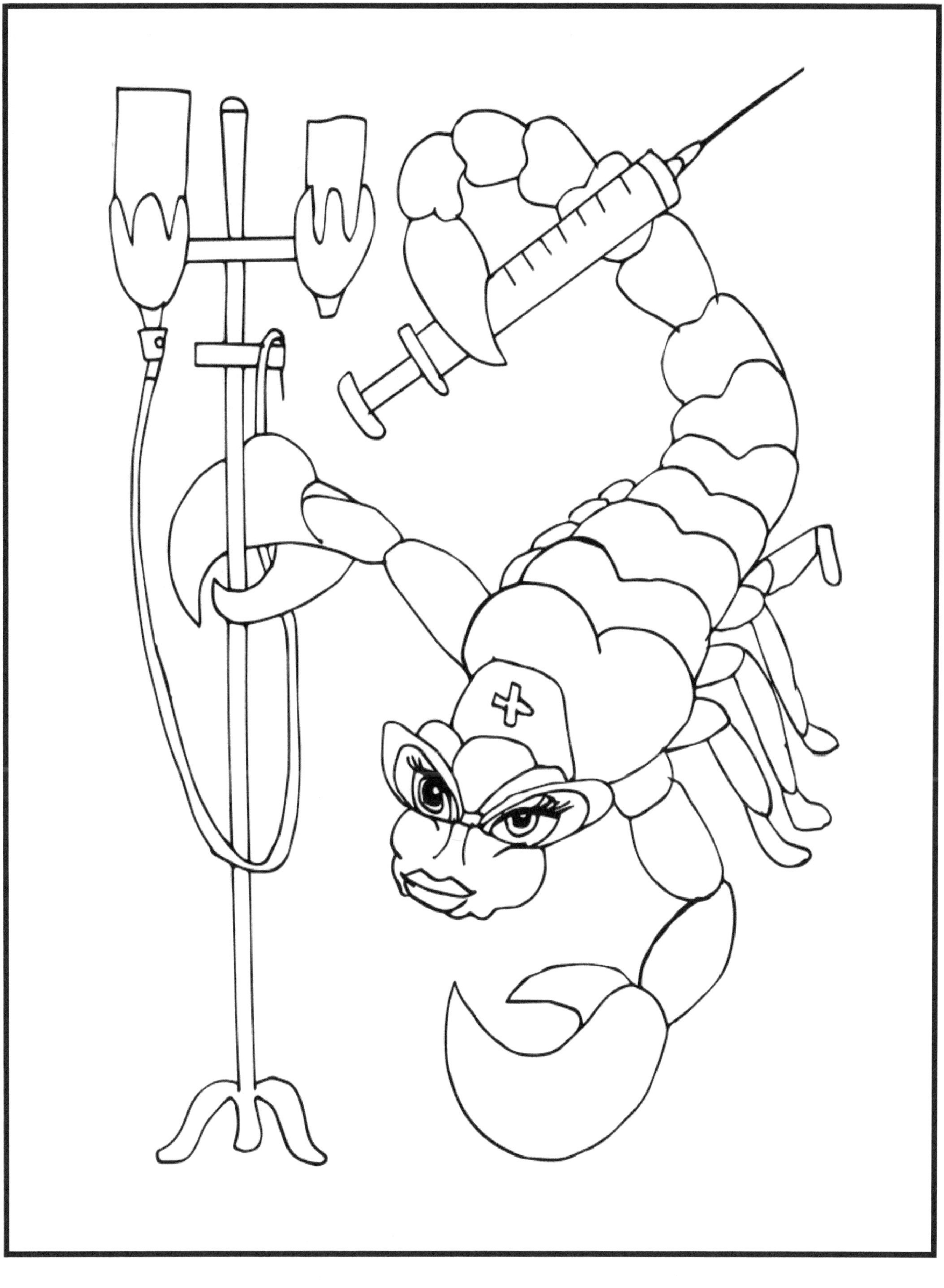

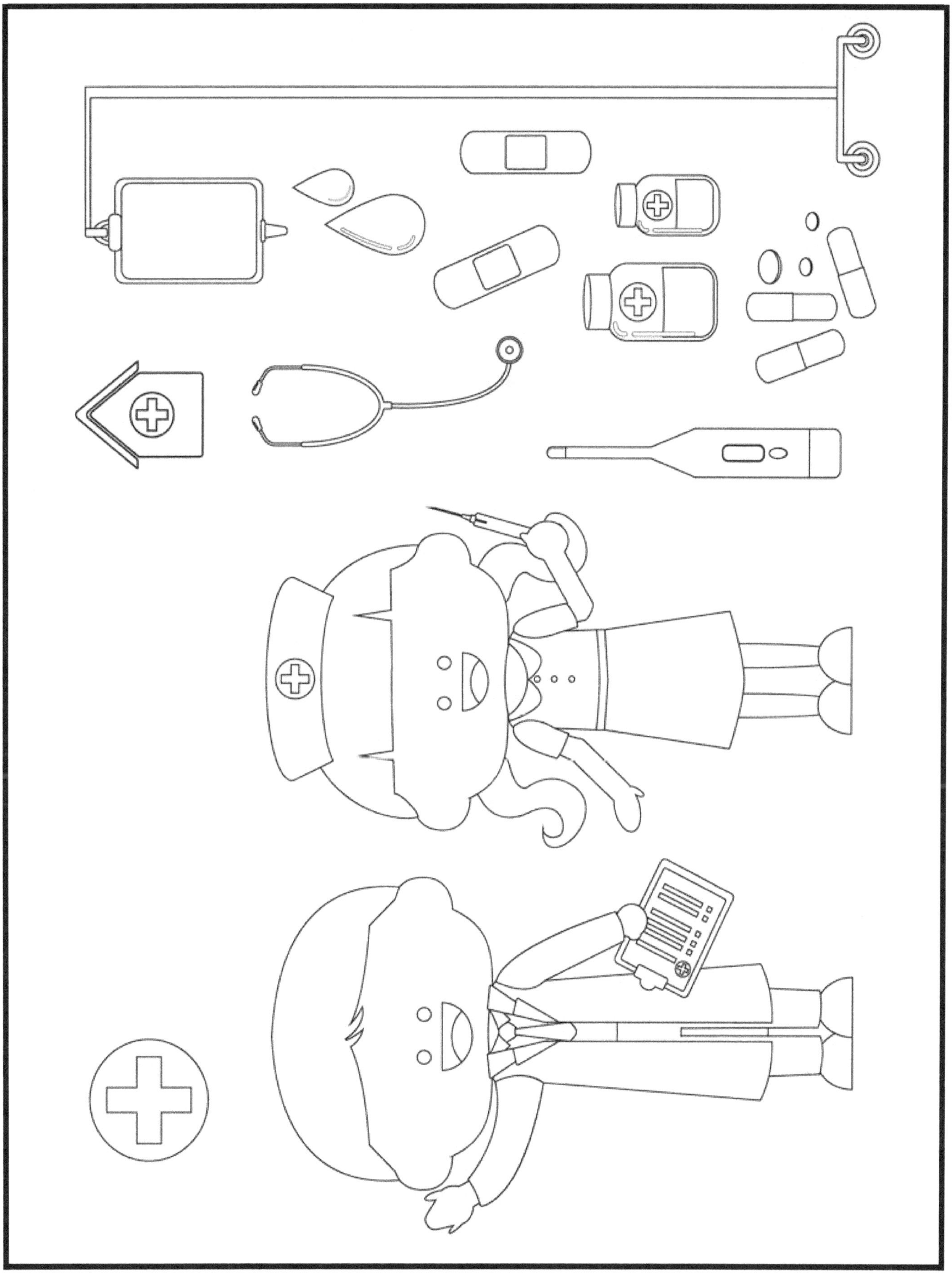

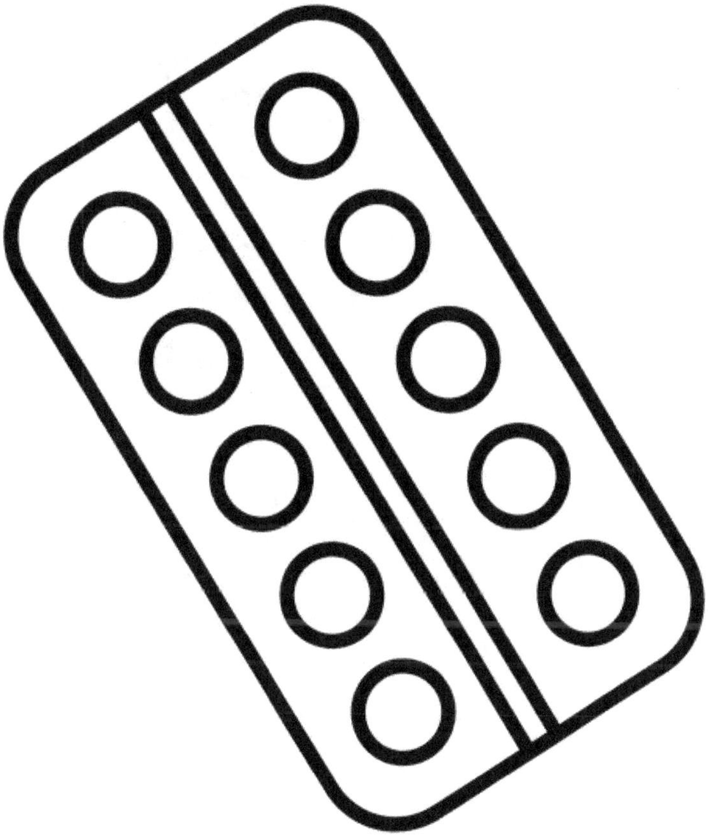

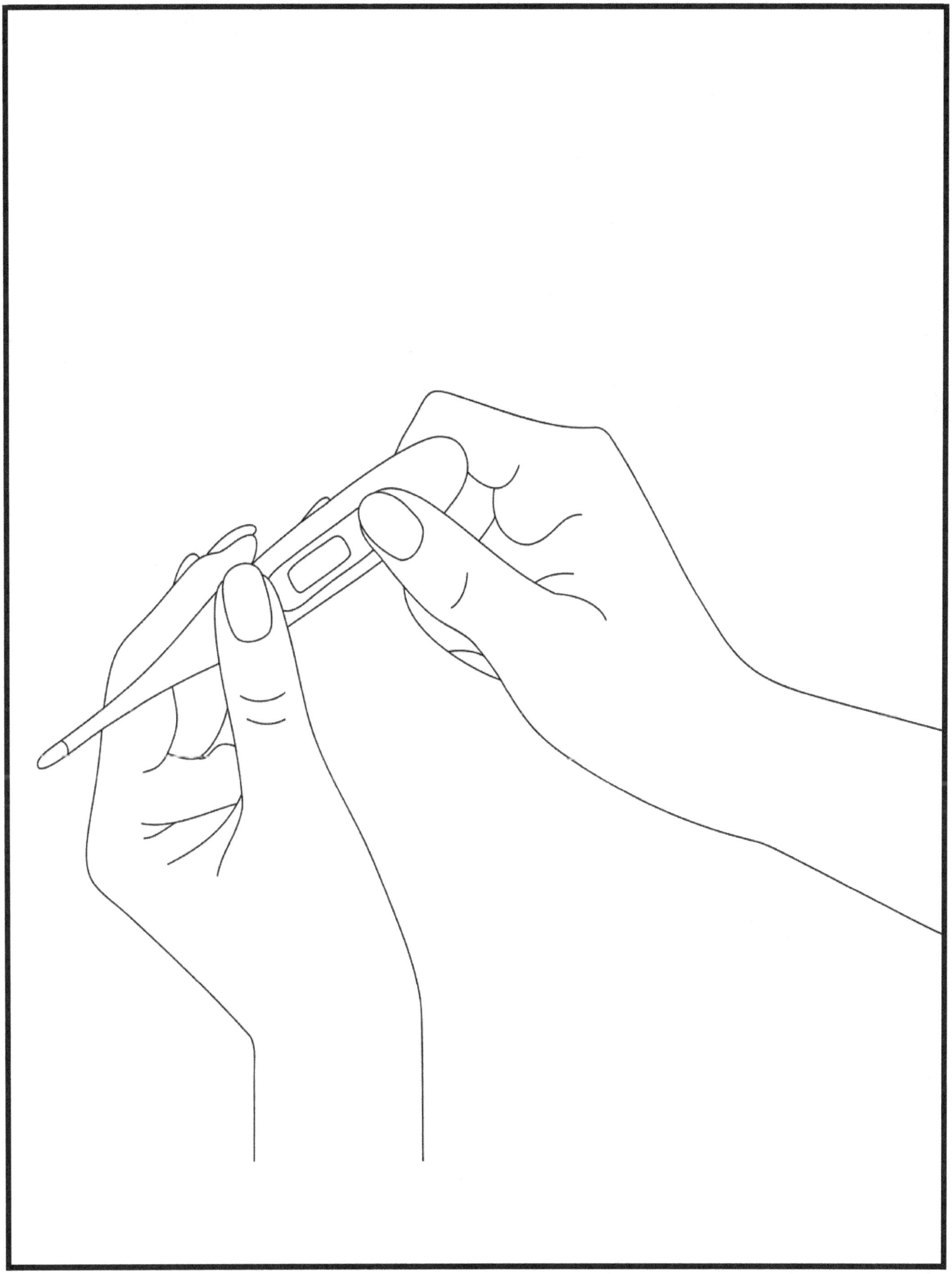

EMERGENCY
AMBULANCE

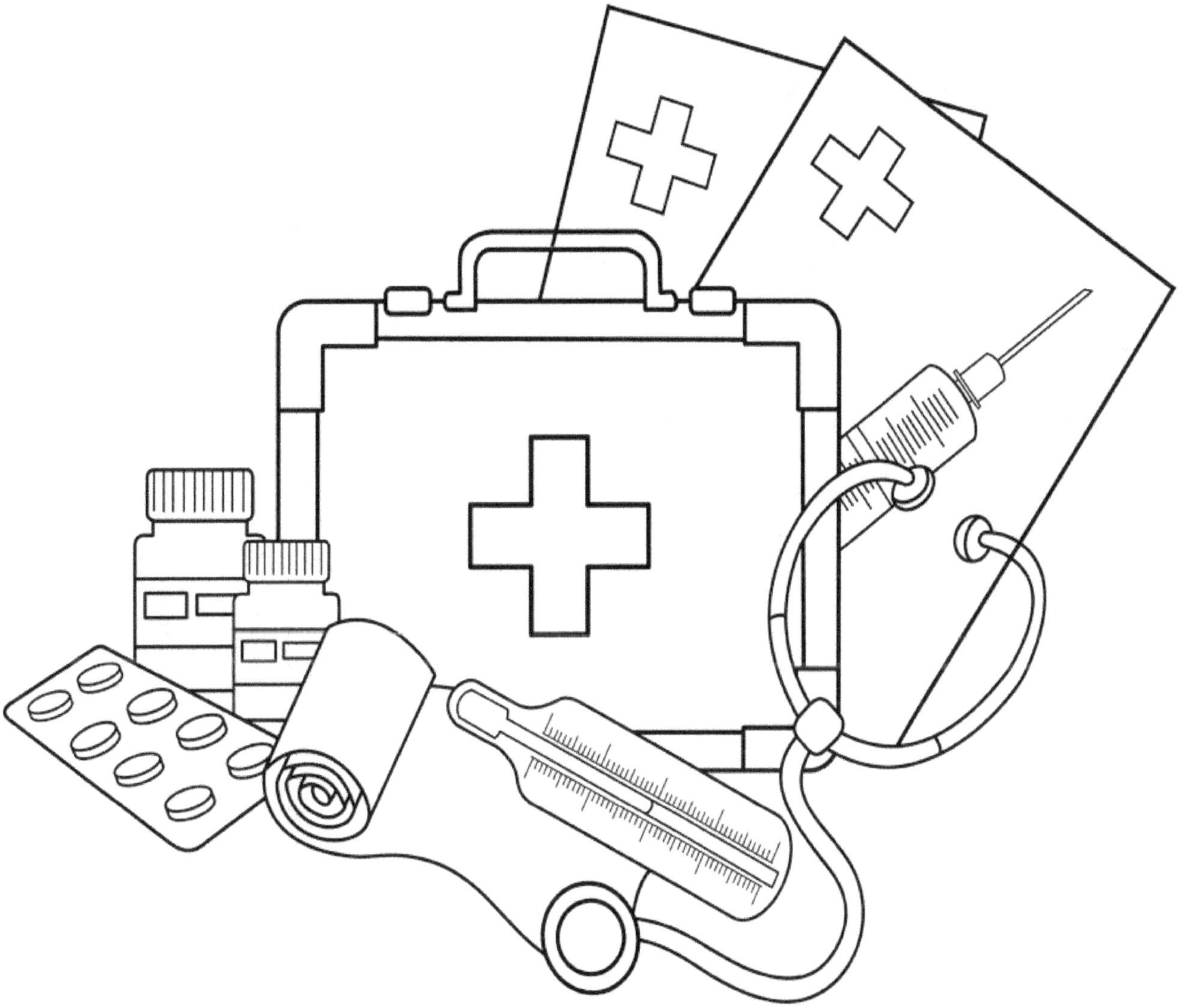

LIFE
SAFE

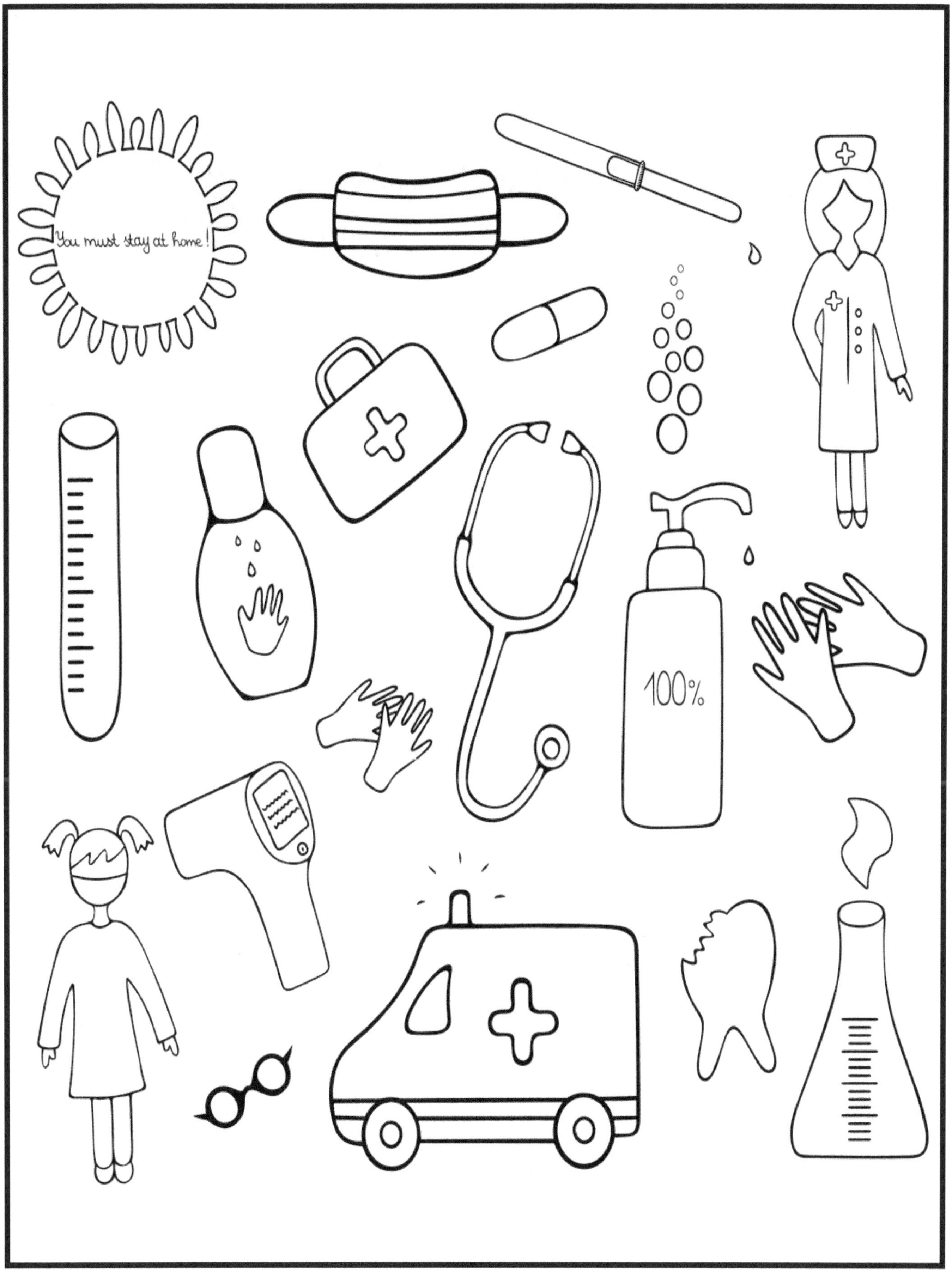
You must stay at home!
100%

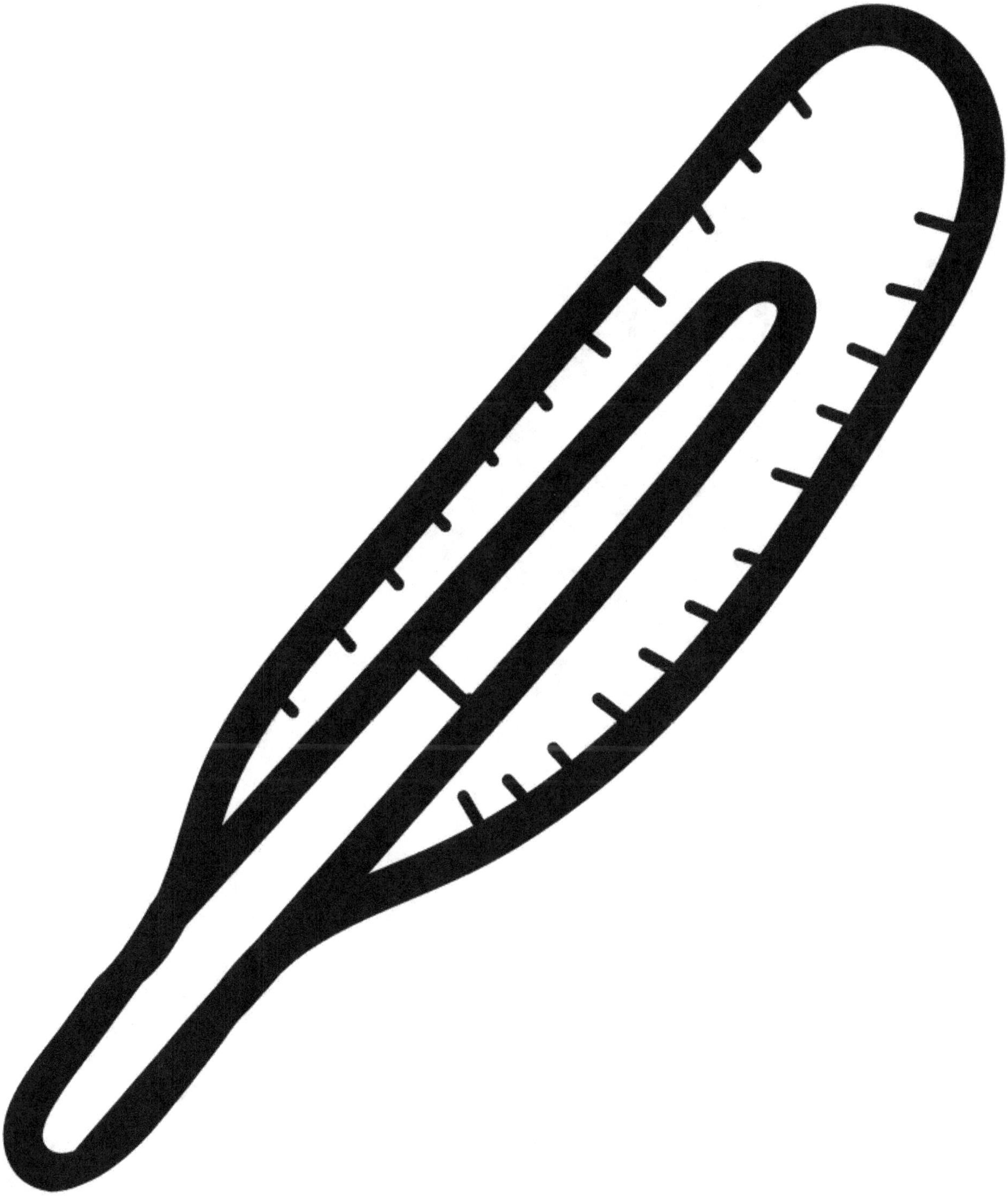

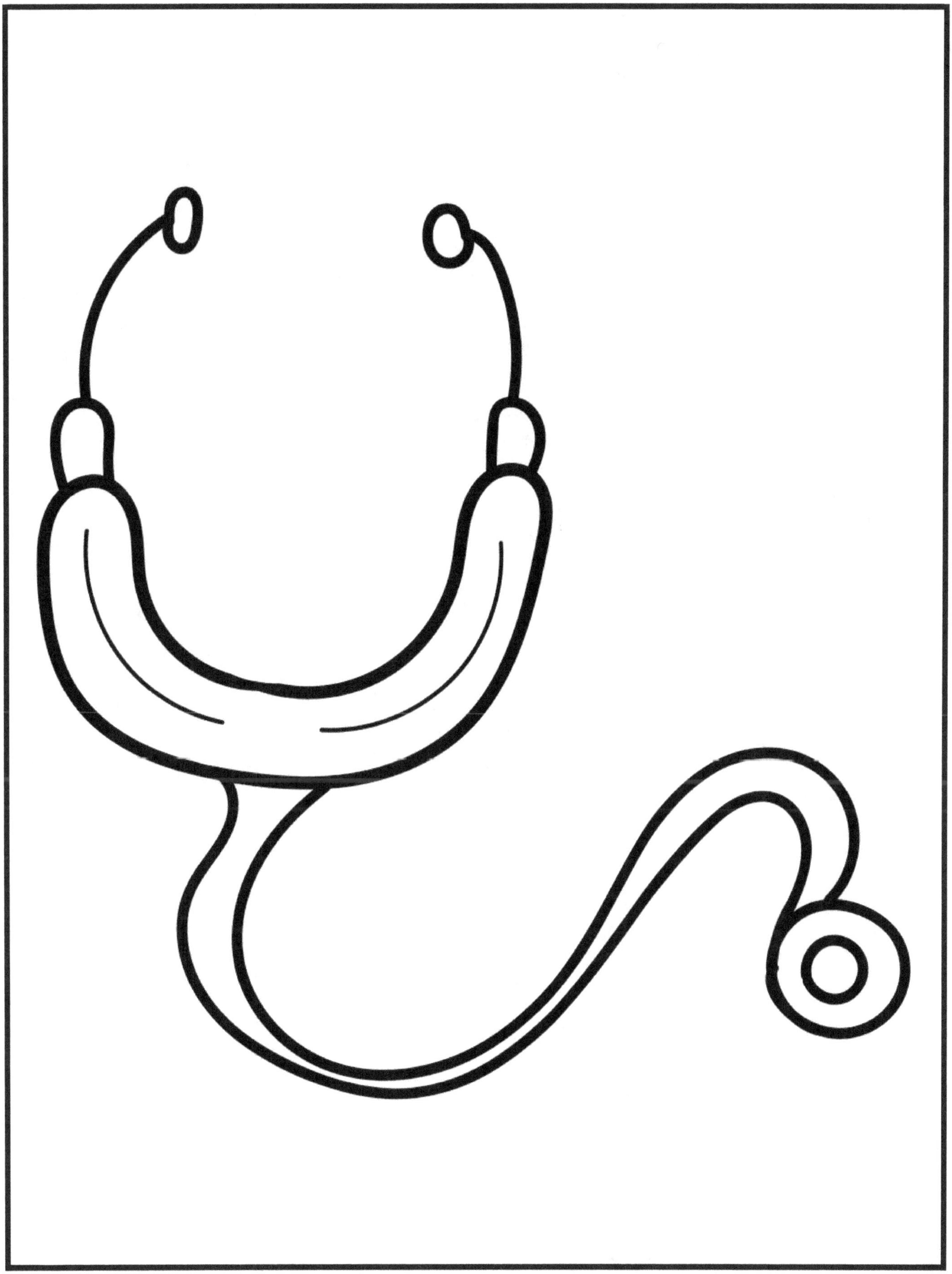

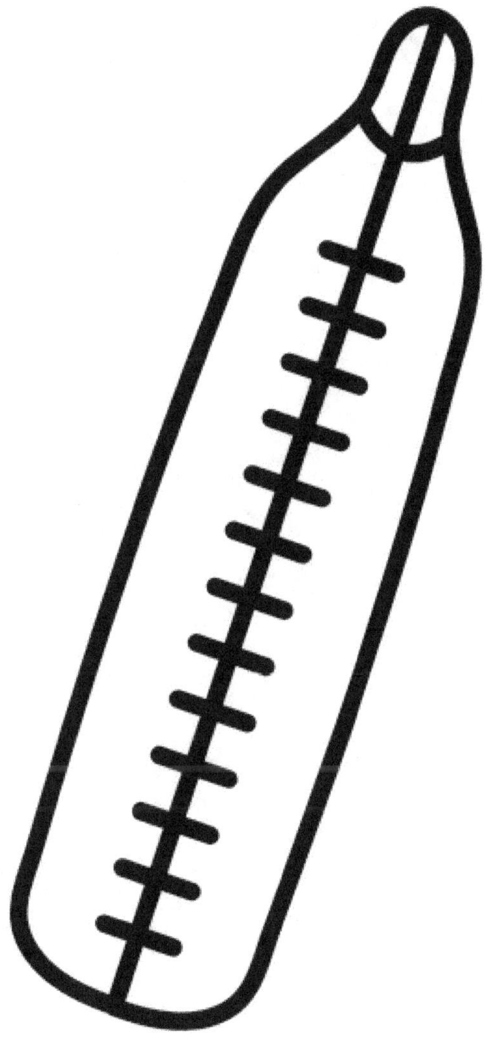

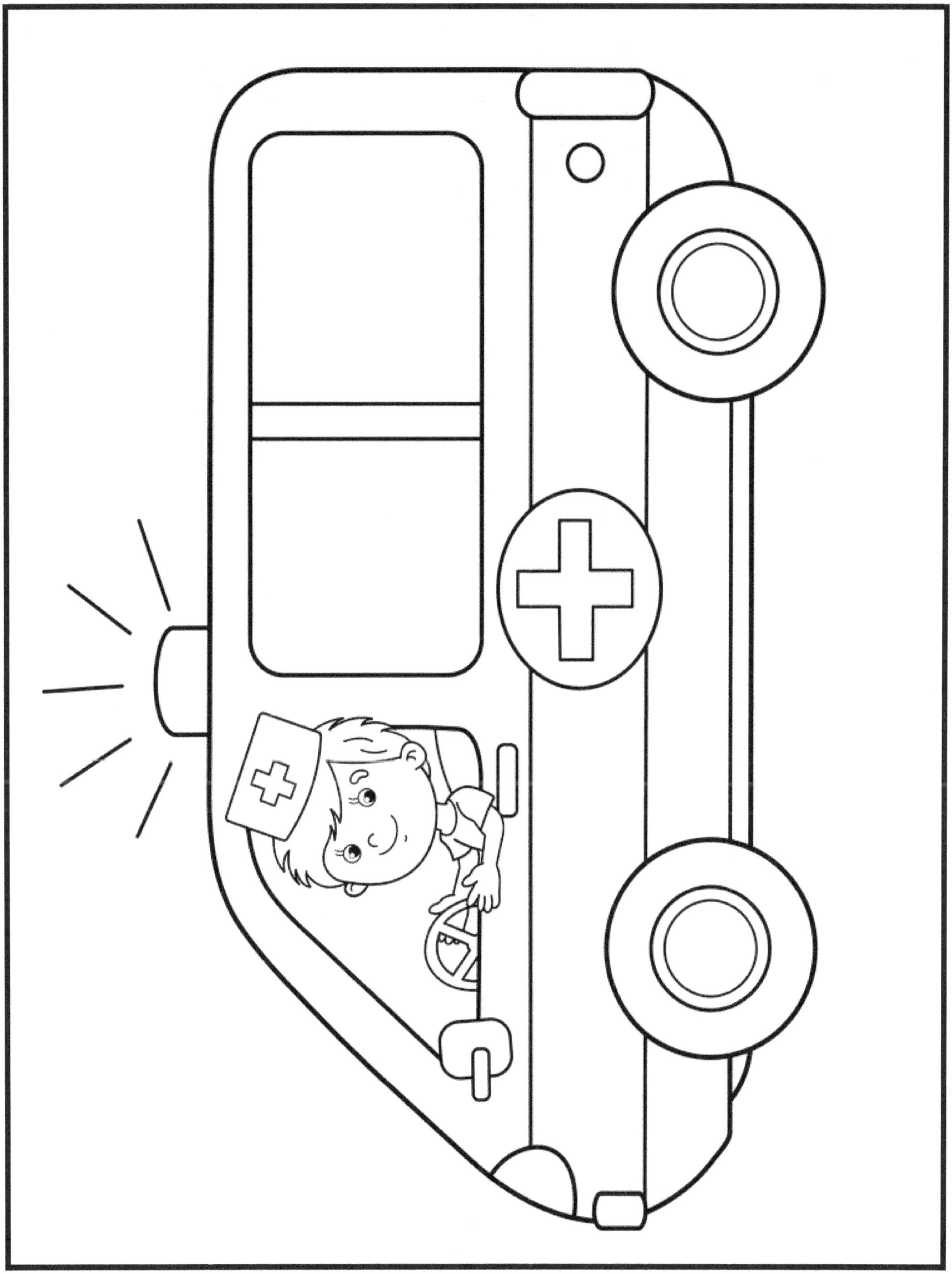

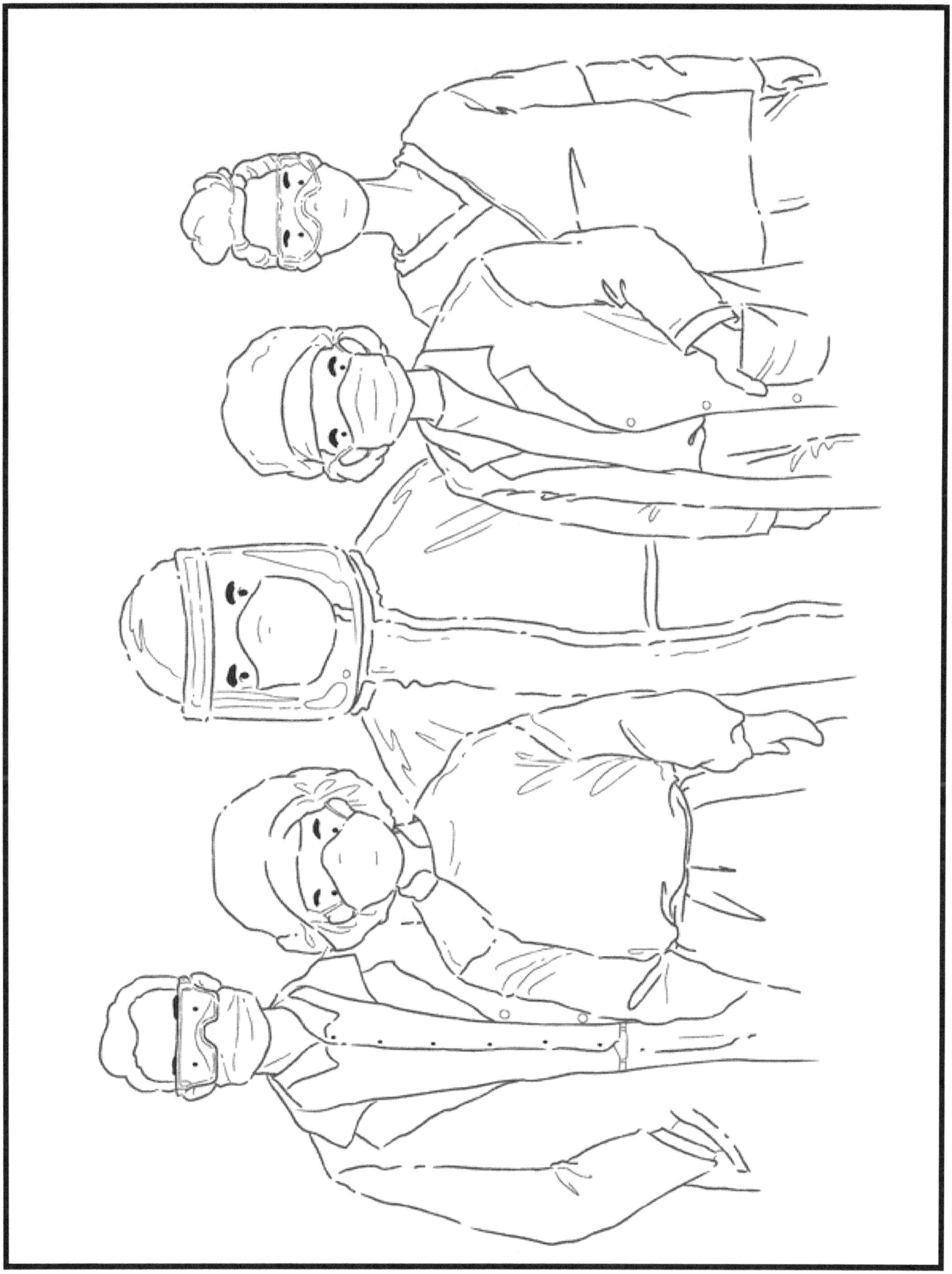

AMBULANCE

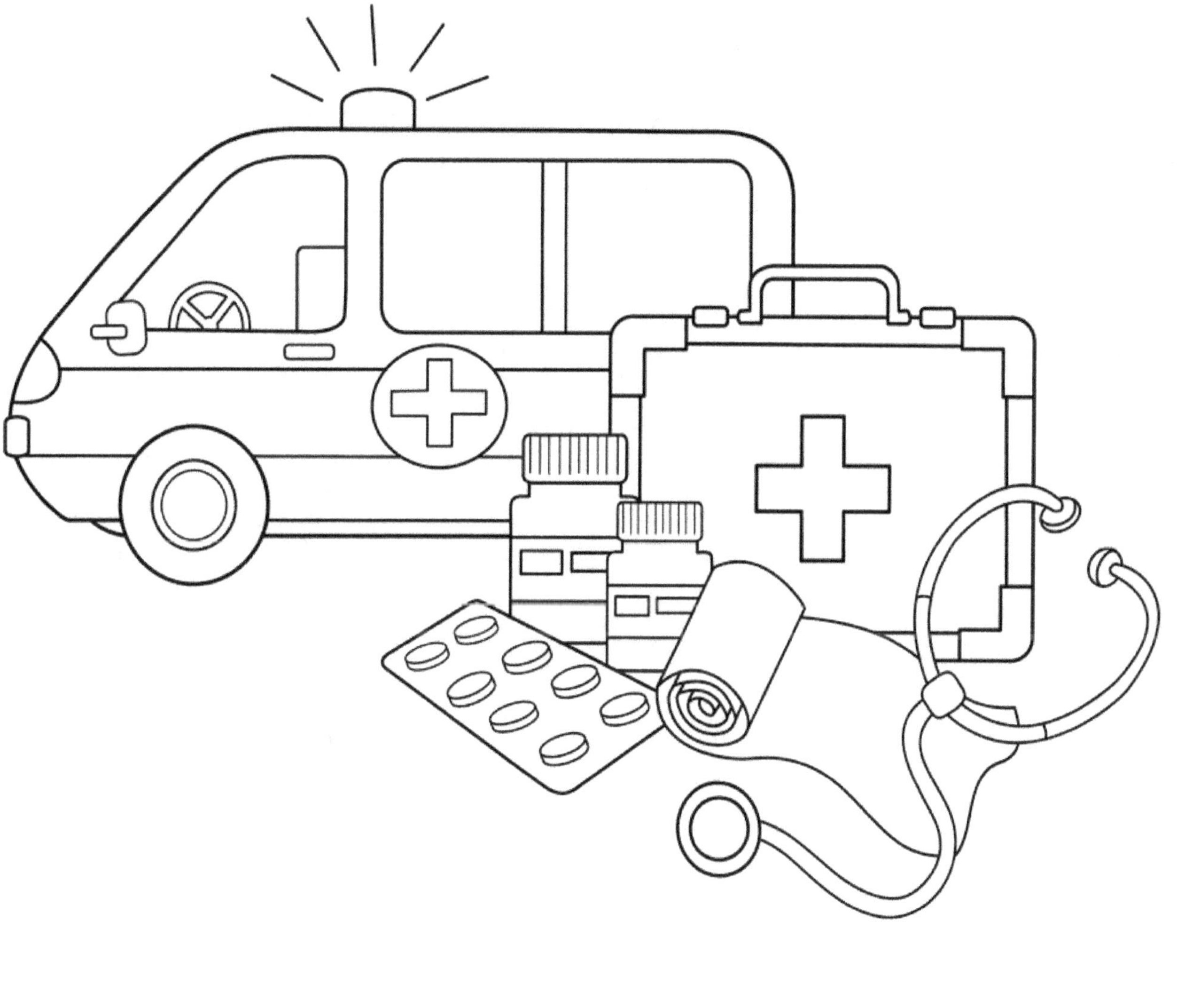

HOSPITAL

THANK
YOU

www.ingramcontent.com/pod-product-compliance
Lightning Source LLC
Chambersburg PA
CBHW081519220526
45467CB00010B/2983
9798715363312